GUIDE TO MAKE YOUR COMPANY SUCCEED: A step-by-step procedure to establish your small-size business.

Donald Watkins

Table of Contents

Chapter 1

Taking the initial step in your business

Steps to starting your business

Starting a company includes planning, making critical financial choices, and completing 0a number of legal processes. Continue reading to learn about each step

Conduct market research

Market research can inform you whether there's a potential to convert your concept into a profitable company. It's a technique to obtain information about possible clients and companies currently functioning in your region. Use the knowledge to discover a competitive advantage for your firm.

Write your business plan

Your business plan is the basis of your company. It's a guide for how to organize, operate, and develop your new firm. You'll use it to persuade others that working with you — or investing in your business — is a wise option.

Fund your business

Your business plan will help you figure out how much money you'll need to launch your firm. If you don't have that amount on hand, you'll need to either raise or borrow the funds. Fortunately, there are more methods than ever to get the financing you need.

Pick your business location

Your company location is one of the most essential choices you'll make. Whether you're starting up a brick-and-mortar company or opening an online shop, the decisions you make might affect your taxes, legal obligations, and earnings.

Choose a business structure

The legal structure you pick for your firm will affect your business registration requirements, how much you pay in taxes, and your liabilities.

Choose your business name

It's not simple to choose the ideal name. You'll want one that matches your brand and captures your personality. You'll also want to check sure your company name isn't already being used by someone else.

Register your business

Once you've found the right company name, it's time to make it official and protect your brand. If you're operating the business under a name different from your own, you'll need to register with the federal government, and maybe your state government, too.

Get federal and state tax IDs
You'll need your employer identification number (EIN) for critical activities to establish and expand your company, such as opening a bank account and paying taxes. It's like a social security number for your company. Some — but not all — states need you to acquire a tax ID as well.

Apply for licenses and permissions
Keep your company functioning smoothly by being legally compliant. The licenses and permissions you require for your

company will vary by industry, state, location, and other considerations.

Open a business bank account

A small company checking account may assist you with legal, tax, and day-to-day difficulties. The good news is it's simple to put one up if you have the necessary registrations and documentation available.

Open Shop

Congratulations! It's time to cut the big ribbon. Your company is officially open. Now, concentrate on maintaining and expanding your company

Chapter 2

Remain Motivated

The sheer possibility of stagnation should be enough to bring your entrepreneur-motivating mojo back online. If that's not enough, here are eight tips for you to get inspired while you expand your company.

1. Recognize That Business Motivation Doesn't Last on Its Own

Ironically, the first step in remaining motivated is acknowledging that inspiration doesn't last—at least not without some effort. Think about the verbs connected with motivation, such as "incite," "stimulate," and "inspire." They all allude to raising something low.

Highs and lows, ebbs and flows, are all cyclical. There are days when you have so much you want to achieve that you won't have the hours. On others, you may struggle to even get dressed. As with every area of your company, inspiration demands ongoing attention and nurturing. So, don't despair at those moments you feel bottomed out. Recall the nearly crazy joy you receive when your entrepreneurial drive appears to be unstoppable and focus on recapturing it.

Motivation neither merely happens nor lasts. It needs attention, determination, and purposeful effort. When it lags, roll up your sleeves, take a task, and go back to the business-building at hand.

2. Expand Your Network

No firm or entrepreneur can function in a bubble. Connection to customers, suppliers, staff, and other entrepreneurs is crucial to building a firm. It's also motivating. I think that one of the things that get me most motivated about my career is the relationships I make when networking.

Networking successfully is about give and take, which means you only receive as good as you give. Be generous with your thoughts, ideas, and connections, and others will reciprocate.

Get the Best Productivity Tools
If you want to be more organized, focused, and motivated, you need some handy toolkits to help you get there.

Whether it's time or satisfaction that you desire more from life, we can assist. Just choose what you need!

Start Taking Action

These days, there are various networking avenues to select from. There are the tried-and-true conventions, industry and professional associations, and even your local Chamber of Commerce. But the internet and social media have dramatically enlarged the opportunity to interact with other empire-building, ambitious individuals.

If you aren't networking because you didn't believe it was worth your time, go out there. Not only will you pick up some amazing ideas, but you'll also find yourself reinspired. Few things are as inspiring as discovering other people's excitement for your company.

3. Focus on Your Goals

We all know that objectives are vital. If we fail to establish them, how do we know when we have done something? In business, like in life, we need objectives.
For me, having a goal focus is naturally motivating. Have you fulfilled all the business targets you established previously? Then, it's time to establish some fresh and even more ambitious ones than before.

Keep in mind that corporate objectives may be changing targets, as circumstances change and reality comes in. What you must avoid is letting yourself or your company be immobilized by indecision.

As Yogi Berra observed, "You've got to be very careful if you don't know where you're going because you might not get there."

The sheer act of making objectives is stimulating, so employ the process when you're at a low. Make sure you establish reasonable goals—neither too lofty nor too low. Once the key ones are in place, set mileposts so you know your firm is on the correct road.

4. Stay True to Your Mission (or Find a New One)

Unlike objectives, the purpose of your organization should not be a shifting target. While a mission may and should be revisited frequently, it must, however, be a constant for a substantial amount of time.

That's because it should be driving everything you do.

The world evolves swiftly. Customers, technology, markets, workforces, and supply chains are in a perpetual state of transformation. In my company, the difficulty has always been to adjust to change while keeping faithful to our objective. On this point, Jim Collins' Hedgehog Concept is dead on.

According to Collins, your goal may be established at the junction of three fundamental realities about your enterprise:

What you're passionately enthusiastic about What you can be greatest in the world at
What powers your economic or resource engine

You should find inspiration in the objective of your organization. If you don't, maybe you aren't enthusiastic about it, can't be the greatest in the world at it, or aren't generating money providing it. If that's the case, find a goal that connects, and you'll recover your entrepreneurial drive.

5. Celebrate Wins and Learn From Losses

Too many times, company owners neglect to appreciate triumphs and learn from setbacks. That's terrible since both victories and losses are two well-known secrets of entrepreneur motivation. If you aren't treating them as the motivators they are, you should be.

Go back to the objectives you established when you began your company. Have you accomplished them?

If you did, have you taken the time to celebrate those victories with your stakeholders? If you haven't attained them, find out why, make modifications, and strive to transform them into victories. Wallowing in defeats instead of learning from them and moving on is a definite way to lose drive.

Don't forget to appreciate the tiny triumphs as well. In my firm, we strike a gong every time we get a new customer so the modest triumph reverberates across the workplace. Doing this boosts our confidence, produces passion, and pushes our team to aspire higher. I advocate creating your technique to appreciate the minor triumphs that are important to create the large victories your organization needs to prosper.

When a lack of drive creeps in, take stock of what you have done. Pat yourself on the back and revel in the glory of success. That pause may be all you need to drive you to attain further accomplishment.

6. Identify Your Disruptive Powers

When you established your company, were you merely joining the pack? Or did you wish to fill a yawning, unfilled market niche? Odds are, you felt you had a solution to an issue that no other firm was finding out.

Take Uber, Netflix, and Blue Apron. They disrupted the taxi, movie, and food sectors by putting a novel twist on the customary manner of conducting business. In doing so, they addressed challenges the market wasn't even aware it had.

The firm you're establishing may not be the next Tesla, but that doesn't mean it can't disrupt an industry, a sector, or simply your local business community. You could uncover a new customer service model or a method to leverage technology that no one else has.

You can't be inventive without being driven, and if you aren't motivated, your firm will only attain the status quo. So, start envisioning ways you may disrupt your sector to restart your drive. Even tiny ripples might evolve into big waves.

7. Spend Some Time Away

Building a company is demanding during regular times. Throw in the stress and profound changes preceding a worldwide epidemic, and life may become overwhelming. This may lead to despair, hesitation, paralysis, or even outright fear.

You can't control the environment, but you can control your reaction to what's occurring. Start by ceasing your efforts to complete it all and establish some priorities instead. When overburdened with life, one of those priorities must be yourself.
Spend some time away from work to refresh. A little rest is the only way you can replenish the vitality and imagination depleted by a tumultuous environment. Work to resist the idea that your company can't function without you, particularly

when your lack of desire isn't doing it any favors anyhow.

A little rest and leisure may be all you need to return to the workplace rejuvenated. If your holiday incorporates travel, exposure to diverse locations and cultures could even generate fresh lines of thinking. You will be encouraged to start up where you left off and go back to expanding your company.

8. Remain Customer-Centric

Whatever widget or widget service you offer, you have consumers. Your lack of drive does a disservice to a market looking to your firm for answers. When your business drive wanes, think about those clients who depend on you to succeed.

Keeping your eye on your consumers isn't a distraction from expanding your company. The most successful organizations in the world are tremendously customer-centric. Think of Apple's amazing ability to predict consumer wants or Google's cloud-based growth deriving from empathy for the issues confronting its customers.

Perhaps, there is a link between your lack of drive and customer neglect. Remaining alert about their demands will decide whether or not your firm is successful. To conduct surveys, study consumer evaluations, and execute market research to find their demands. After all, if you aren't fixing their issues, what are you doing?

When the noise from the everyday responsibilities of operating a company becomes too loud, tune it out. Listen to what your consumers are saying about you and what they're asking for. Responding to them will need attention since you are driven by your ambition to develop a great firm.

Final Thoughts

Motivation is movement and action—a driving force of human nature. Although it waxes and wanes as naturally as the moon cycle, reviving the business drive might need a deliberate effort. It's an effort you'll want to make since a prolonged lack of drive is fatal.

If you lack the drive to eat, you starve. If you lack the urge to drive in your lane, you crash. If you lack the drive to create your company, you fail.

You are a very driven guy. If you weren't, you never would have launched a company of your own. Entrepreneurs are, at their heart, a rare and particularly inspired breed.

So, when your entrepreneurial motivation flatlines, don't quit. Whether the spark comes from a personal connection, a new objective, a quick vacation, or a client remark, there are methods to get yourself back on the business-building road again.

Chapter 3

Remember the core business focus

Steps to Help You Stay Focused During Your Business Growth.
When your firm is expanding, so are your obligations.
Some firms that began tiny are now on their road to becoming worldwide. This type of progress is excellent, but developing a firm is not simple.

Some entrepreneurs may feel a bit overwhelmed as they seek to push the accelerator. This is because various variables, including sales and revenue performance, personal problems, and even the social atmosphere, may all add to their stress and be perceived as hurdles to their firms' success.

There are various reasons why your attention is fading, so don't be worried if you can't explain what's causing your lack of concentration on any specific job when your company is developing.

Finding concentration is a difficulty that everyone experiences.

I know personally how tough it is to stay attentive. However, if you keep focused on your objectives and weather bad times, you can make it through. You merely need to be nimble and adapt to the changing environment but not lose sight of your company objectives.

Here are 5 basic methods on how to keep focused amid your company's quick growth:

1. Manage just the things you can manage

This is a truth for all of us: we have no control over many things that happen in our life.

It's quite simple for the mind to overthink when trying to take in everything you can't control.

If you push yourself to avoid these things from occurring, your mind will be flooded with worry and tension - you'll merely spend your time and energy on them.

Instead, why not concentrate your efforts on a few areas you can control?

According to research by Microsoft Research, individuals who seek to concentrate on more than one item at a time lose their productivity by up to 40%.

That is why you need to focus on the things you can only count on with your hands. Determine what you can control first, and then search for answers to those problems.

I assure you that you will begin to make more favorable selections if you learn to master what you can manage to control throughout your company's quick expansion. Besides, after learning it, you may execute positive and empowered activities for your company objectives.

2. Be mindful of your triggers

We can't always avoid all distractions. Opposing opinions could be one thing or even a challenges to our egos. That occurs, and it varies based on the scenario.

Our thoughts, experiences, and memories are all related to triggers. We link our history with analogous emotional triggers and the present condition.

According to Lifehack, there are three frequent symptoms for which you should either create boundaries:

Guilt Discomfort Resentment
But before you can create limits, the first step to remaining focused is to look deep

inside yourself to identify why you're losing concentration in the first place.

Then, using self-observation and insight, you may determine your boundary cues.

This way, if you are aware of your triggers and establish limits, you have a more significant chance to put the required mechanisms in place to minimize your exposure to distractions dramatically.

Just concentrate on the things you need to complete - self-management is a wonderful approach as it helps us to control our emotions so that they don't interfere with our job.

3. Get back to your 'why'

Getting back to our mission is a fantastic wake-up call.

When unplanned setbacks derail our company goals or stop our growth strategy, we lose our concentration to remain on course.

What you need to do is simply breathe and take a step back.

Get back to your "why".

According to Simon Sinek, the 'Why' message is possibly the most essential message that an organization or person can communicate as it drives people to action.

A powerful and positive purpose statement can assist you traverse hard times and murky seas.

It's also time to build processes that are functionally aligned with your mission.

These techniques, if used successfully, will not only aid you but also your teams and may drive the development of your business like wildfire.

4. Avoid or reduce digital distractions

If you're easily distracted by your phone, laptop, or computer alerts, you're not alone.
Digital gadgets have become more and more of a distracting factor.

Nir Eyal, a technology and psychology expert and author of Indistractable: How to Control Your Attention and Choose

Your Life, says that the reason why individuals desire to become diverted is to escape pain and discomfort at the neurological level.

So, when we're presented with a tough aim or target we don't want to attain, we hunt for a distraction, which is easy to acquire by these days using digital technology.

With these digital distractions, you only have a limited period for deep thought and flow states, essential for complicated work necessitating distraction-free attention.

You may apply these tactics in your career or even at home to remain focused:

Utilize peaceful spaces
Screen your phone calls and answer only critical calls

Minimise phone notifications

Organise and arrange undisturbed concentration time

Take phone-free breaks

Limit email and message checking

Remove social media applications that are no longer required

With these workplace methods, you may eliminate digital distractions and discover new ways to become more productive and remain more focused throughout work hours.

5. Create a daily 'to-do' list and stick to it

Are you sure that you know what you're expected to accomplish for the day? Or for the week?

When organizing your days, make sure you understand the tasks you'll be performing and what it will take to finish them.

Sometimes, when you keep adding items to your list, things may start to go wrong. As a consequence, you can wind yourself up hurrying things. Moreover, some of the chores that you've put on your list could be hard to accomplish in one day.

If this is the case, this was probably the biggest cause of your stress throughout the day, leading you to lose sight of your goals.

Having a simplified 'to-do' list is necessary, particularly for key operations, since you will be able to advance the most significant business goals for your company's development.

Personal productivity starts with a decent to-do list. Finding a task-management program and technique that works for you a tremendous relief, such as Asana, Monday, Trello, and the like.

Remember, establish a "to-do" list with the most crucial chores at the top and the least important at the bottom.

Creating a great task list needs some practice. Things will look a lot nicer, and you will be more productive overall once you learn to put all the elements together.

When you've achieved all the "done" chores, you'll experience a feeling of achievement and pleasure to retain your focus as your business expands.

Chapter 4

Setting a smart business strategy

How to Write a Business Plan, Step by Step
A well-written business plan should contain facts about your organization's focus, goods or services, and finances.

STEPS

1. Write an executive summary
2. Describe your business
3. State your business objectives
4. Describe your goods and services
5. Do your market research
6. Outline your marketing and sales strategy

7. Perform a company financial analysis
8. Make financial estimates
9. Add new material to an appendix

A business plan is a document that details your firm's financial objectives and discusses how you'll reach them. A robust, thorough strategy will create a road map for the business's next three to five years, and you may share it with prospective investors, lenders, or other crucial partners.

Here's a step-by-step approach to drafting your business plan.

1. Write an executive summary
This is the first page of your company strategy. Think of it as your elevator pitch. It should contain a goal statement, a short explanation of the items or services

supplied, and a general outline of your financial development ambitions.

Though the executive summary is the first thing your investors will read, it might be simpler to write it last. That way, you may emphasize facts you've recognized while writing other parts that go into greater depth.

2. Describe your business

Next up is your business description, which should include information like:

Your business's registered name.
Address of your company location.
Names of prominent persons in the company. Make sure to showcase distinct abilities or technical competence among members of your team.

Your company description should also explain your business structure — such as a sole proprietorship, partnership, or corporation — and indicate the percent ownership that each owner has and the level of each owner's engagement in the firm.

Lastly, it should address the history of your organization and the nature of your business currently. This prepares the reader to learn about your aims in the following part.

3. State your business objectives

The third section of a business strategy is a goal statement. This part explains precisely what you'd want to achieve, both in the short term and over the long run.

If you're searching for a business loan or outside investment, you may use this part to describe why you have a clear need for the cash, how the finance will help your firm expand, and how you expect to reach your growth ambitions. The objective is to offer a clear description of the potential provided and how the loan or investment can expand your firm.

For example, if your firm is establishing a second product line, you may describe how the loan would assist your company launch the new product and how much you estimate sales will rise over the following three years as a consequence.

4. Describe your goods and services
In this area, go into depth about the items or services you provide or intend to offer.

You should include the following:

A description of how your product or service works.
The price model for your product or service.
The average clientele you service.
Your supply chain and order fulfillment strategy.
Your sales plan.
Your distribution plan.

You may also discuss existing or pending trademarks and patents linked with your product or service.

5. Do your market research

Lenders and investors will want to know what makes your product distinct from your competitors. In your market analysis section, describe who your rivals are.

Discuss what they do well, and point out what you can do better. If you're servicing a separate or underserved market, explain that.

6. Outline your marketing and sales strategy

Here, you might address how you aim to convince clients to acquire your goods or services, or how you will establish customer loyalty that will lead to repeat business.

7. Perform a company financial analysis

If you're a startup, you may not have much information about your firm financials yet. However, if you're an established firm, you'll want to include income or profit-and-loss statements, a balance sheet that includes your assets and obligations, and a cash flow statement that illustrates how cash comes into and goes out of the organization.

You may also add metrics such as:

Net profit margin: the proportion of revenue you retain as net income.
Current ratio: the gauge of your liquidity and capacity to repay obligations.
Accounts receivable turnover ratio: a measurement of how often you collect on receivables each year.

This is a fantastic location to incorporate charts and graphs that make it simple for individuals reading your plan to comprehend the financial health of your organization.

8. Make financial estimates

This is a vital aspect of your company strategy if you're seeking finance or investors. It details how your firm will create enough profit to repay the loan or how you will make a good return for investors.

Here, you'll enter your business's monthly or quarterly sales, costs, and profit predictions over at least three years — with the future figures assuming you've acquired a fresh loan.

Accuracy is crucial, so thoroughly study your prior financial data before offering estimates. Your objectives may be ambitious, but they should also be reasonable.

9. Add new material to an appendix

List any supporting information or supplementary items that you couldn't fit in elsewhere, such as resumes of key personnel, licenses, equipment leases, permits, patents, receipts, bank statements, contracts, and personal and company credit history. If the appendix is large, you may want to consider adding a table of contents at the beginning of this section.

Business plan advice and resources
Here are some suggestions to make your business plan stand out:

Avoid over-optimism: If you're looking for a business loan at a local bank, the loan officer likely understands your market very well. Providing excessive sales predictions will jeopardize your chances of loan approval.

Proofread: Spelling, punctuation, and grammatical issues may pop off the page and turn off lenders and potential investors, taking their emphasis off your company and placing it on the faults you made. If writing and editing aren't your strong suit, you may choose to employ a professional business plan writer, copy editor, or proofreader.

Use free resources: SCORE is a nonprofit group that provides a broad network of volunteer business mentors and professionals that can assist you draft or update your business plan. You may seek a mentor or locate a local SCORE chapter for extra advice.

The U.S. Small Business Administration's Small Business Preparation Centers, which give free business advice and aid with business plan preparation, might also be a resource.

Chapter 5

Dedication to your business

Steps to Becoming a More Passionate, Dedicated Entrepreneur

In the corporate world, it requires both enthusiasm and determination to reach the top.

I've heard time and time again that anybody can become an entrepreneur. For the most part, I find this to be accurate. At any given moment, at least one person I know is attempting to start a company. Some of these people achieve success, while others discover that entrepreneurship is a long and arduous path that fails.

Why do I bring this up in a piece on being a more passionate, driven entrepreneur, though? While everybody can "do" entrepreneurship, not everyone can do it successfully. To flourish as an entrepreneur, you'll need to work harder for your enterprise than you've ever done in your life.

If you want to establish or expand your own company but presently lack this level of drive, you've come to the correct spot. Below, you'll discover measures you may take to become a more passionate, devoted entrepreneur.

Change your viewpoint
Your working life is made of around 80,000 hours. This is a vast chunk of time with endless choices, yet curiously

enough, there's one frequent sort of advice -- pursue your passion.

On the surface, this seems like excellent counsel. As you dive a little farther into it, however, it may begin to unravel. What if you don't know what you're enthusiastic about? What if you believe you're enthusiastic about something, but others appear to have greater enthusiasm for the same thing? As it turns out, this widespread practice doesn't always make sense.

So, instead of concentrating on passion, concentrate on how you can be significant. Try to discover something that has a bigger influence than financial ROI. Of course, you may still have a career in entrepreneurship that's incredibly rich, but your main objective should still be meaningful employment. To increase your passion, remind yourself that you're contributing to the answer to a serious issue every day.

Don't overcomplicate things

When you identify with something significant, concern could start to creep in. Starting and maintaining your own business is going to make you feel inadequate at times, but this shouldn't stop you back. Regardless of your experience, simply get started. The sooner you start working on your new love, the quicker you'll study more and begin to come an expert in the industry.

As you begin to work with your passion, uncertainty will undoubtedly slip in. You can find yourself caught up in the idea that you don't know whether you'll be able to see the situation through, but try not to become lost in this thinking. Instead, split your job into smaller, more manageable parts. Focus on everyday modest steps that propel you ahead. Before long, you won't be over-complicating things, but properly addressing every duty as it occurs.

Embrace being new.
It's frequently hard for folks to hear that they're incorrect or that they misunderstand something. Being a novice is not easy, but if you can learn to accept that you are a beginner, you'll open yourself up to a world of opportunity.

When you accept your blank slate, you'll be able to learn more about your profession. A huge component of getting passionate is studying. Remember, as a starter, you're in a terrific position to create profound enthusiasm and love for your enterprise.

Cope with failure.

Signing onto a project where failure is practically assured sounds ludicrous, yet numerous entrepreneurs do it every day. Although your life has undoubtedly been structured on avoiding failure, you'll need to embrace it to become a more passionate and determined entrepreneur.

The folks succeeding as entrepreneurs consider failure as a common and acceptable occurrence. When they fail, they find out what went wrong and then they move on. Persevering over tiny faults and concerns is poisonous in business. Luckily, everyone can learn how to perceive failure as a challenge.

Give yourself room.

When everything is said and done, you want your enterprise to complement you, not complete you. Some individuals allow their passion to become a part of who they are, which may inhibit progress. To fully succeed, you'll need to preserve a little autonomy so you can make sensible, objective business choices that take you closer to your objectives.

To guarantee that your enthusiasm does not overwhelm who you are, ask yourself this question every year: "Would an outsider associate my venture with me, or would they say that I am my venture?"

Chapter 6

Cash Formula

How to calculate cash flow: 3 cash flow formulas, calculations, and examples
In principle, cash flow isn't too complicated—it's a reflection of how money goes into and out of your firm.

Unfortunately, for small company owners, understanding and implementing cash flow formulae doesn't always come effortlessly. So much so that 60% of small company owners claim they don't feel informed about accounting or finance. But by taking the time to learn about these three essential cash flow formulas—free cash flow, cash flow from operations, and cash flow forecast—you're on the right route to feeling more confident about your company finances and managing your cash flow.

For small firms in particular, cash flow is one of the most critical factors in their financial health. One research indicated that 30% of firms fail because they run out of money. Using cash flow formulae may help you plan for slow seasons and ensure you have adequate money on hand before investing in your company.

It is vitally essential that any entrepreneur understand what their firm working capital requirements are and plan to secure their capacity to fund development.

Important cash flow formulae to know about:

Free Cash Flow = Net income + Depreciation/Amortization – Change in Working Capital – Capital Expenditure

Operating Cash Flow = Operating Income + Depreciation – Taxes + Change in Working Capital

Cash Flow Forecast = Beginning Cash + Projected Inflows – Projected Outflows = Ending Cash

The three cash flow algorithms above each have their perks and tell you various things about your firm. Don't worry if they appear complex! We'll go through concepts, computations, and examples together.

1. Free cash flow formula

One of the most frequent and essential cash flow formulae is free cash flow (or FCF).

While a standard cash flow statement (like the one you can obtain from Wave reports) offers you a picture of your business's cash at a particular moment, it doesn't always assist with planning and budgeting—because it doesn't represent the cash you have accessible, or free to utilize.

Can you afford to invest in that new software? Do you have enough cash on hand to pay for that virtual assistant when their invoice comes due? How much cash do you have free to spend on thank you cards for your clients?

Calculating the amount you have available to spend (using the FCF formula) helps answer those problems and others like it.

How to calculate free cash flow

Calculating your business's free cash flow is considerably simpler than you would believe. To start, you'll need your firm Income Statement or Balance Sheet to gather crucial financial statistics.

Example of a balance sheet, displaying assets and liabilities.

First, let's get some crucial financial phrases clear.

Net income: The total money left over after you've calculated your company expenditures from overall revenue or sales. You'll find this on your Income Statement.

Depreciation/Amortization: Many of your company assets (like equipment) lose value over time. Depreciation is the measurement of how that value diminishes. Amortization, on the other hand, is a means of breaking down the original cost of an item throughout its lifespan. You'll discover depreciation and amortization on your Income Statement.

Working Capital: Working capital is the gap between your assets and liabilities and reflects the capital utilized in the day-to-day functioning of your firm. You may determine your working capital using the total assets and liabilities on your Balance Sheet.

Capital Expenditure: Capital expenditures comprise money your firm spends on fixed assets, such as land, real estate, or equipment. You may discover your capital expenditure on the Statement of Cash Flows.

With that information in hand, the fundamental calculation for free cash flow looks like this:

Free Cash Flow = Net income + Depreciation/Amortization – Change in Working Capital – Capital Expenditure

Free Cash Flow Example

Let's take a look at an example of that formula in the real world. Randi's a freelance graphic designer—she wants to assess her free cash flow to determine whether employing a virtual assistant for 10 hours a month is financially possible.

Her financials for the year look like this:

Net income = $80,000
Depreciation/Amortization = $0
Change in Working Capital = – $10,000

Capital Expenditure = $2,500 (Randi got a new iMac last year)
So Randi's free cash flow is represented by:

[$80,000] + [$0] – [-$10,000] – [$2,500] = $67,500

That implies she has $67,500 in ready funds to put back into her firm.

2. Operating cash flow formula

Knowing your cash flow from operations is necessary when having an accurate perspective of your cash flow.

While free cash flow offers you a solid understanding of the cash available to reinvest in the firm, it doesn't necessarily present the most accurate picture of your routine, daily cash flow. That's because the FCF formula doesn't account for irregular spending, income, or investing. If you sell off a major asset, your free cash flow would increase considerably up—but it doesn't represent the average cash flow for your organization. When you need a better notion of normal cash flow for your organization, you want to apply the operational cash flow (OCF) formula.

For example, if you're attempting to acquire outside investment from a bank or venture capital company, they're more likely to be interested in your operational cash flow. The same applies if you begin working with an accountant or financial adviser, so it's crucial to understand what OCF looks like for you before obtaining assistance.

How to calculate operating cash flow: Just like with our free cash flow calculation above, you'll want to have your Balance Sheet and Income Statement at the ready, so you can retrieve the data involved in the operating cash flow formula.

There's one additional financial measure you'll need to know for this calculation:

Operating Income: Also called Earnings Before Interest and Taxes (or EBIT) and profit, your operating income subtracts operating expenditures (such as labor paid and cost of products sold) from total revenue. You may discover operational income on your Income Statement.

The fundamental OCF formula is:

Operating Cash Flow = Operating Income + Depreciation − Taxes + Change in Working Capital

A graphic illustrating the indirect approach versus the direct method. Under the indirect approach, there is Net Income; Adjustments (Depreciation and amortization, Changes in working capital); Net cash from the owner; and Activities. Under the direct method, there are collections from consumers; deductions (payments to suppliers, salaries); net cash from operations; and activities.

Operating Cash Flow Example
To apply the cash flow from operations calculation to our previous example (Randi, our favorite freelance graphic designer), let's suppose her financials for the year look like this:

Operating Income = $85,000

Depreciation = $0 Taxes = $9,000

Change in Working Capital = − $10,000

Randi's operational cash flow formula is represented by:

[$85,000] + [$0] − [$9,000] + [-$10,000] = $66,000

That indicates, in a normal year, Randi makes $66,000 in positive cash flow from her regular operational operations.

3. Cash flow forecast formula

While both FCF and OCF offer you a decent understanding of cash flow at a particular time, it isn't necessarily what you need when it comes to budgeting for the future. That's why estimating your cash flow for the following month or quarter is a helpful exercise to help you better grasp how much cash you'll have on hand in the future.

Cash flow difficulties are never enjoyable (remember they're responsible for a significant proportion of small company failures), so it's crucial to guarantee positive cash flow before you start spending.

How to compute your cash flow prediction: Your cash flow forecast is probably one of the simplest formulae to calculate. There aren't any technical financial concepts involved—it's simply a straightforward computation of the cash you plan to come in and spend over (usually) the following 30 or 90 days.

The formula looks like this:

Cash Flow Forecast = Beginning Cash + Projected Inflows – Projected Outflows = Ending Cash

Beginning cash is, of course, how much cash your firm has on hand today—and you can extract that amount directly from your Statement of Cash Flows.

Project inflows are the funds you anticipate receiving during the stated period. That includes current bills that will come due and future invoices you intend to issue and receive payment for.

Project outflows are the spending and other payments you'll make in the provided period.

Getting back to our Randi example, let's imagine she has:

Beginning cash = $30,000

Projected inflows over the next 90 days = $30,000

Project outflows for the next 90 days = $4,000

Here's what her cash flow prediction looks like:

[$30,000] + [$30,000] – [$4,000] = $56,000

That implies Randi's expected cash flow for the following quarter is $56,000.

Cash flow formulas: Math to control your cash flow.

As a small company owner, calculating cash flow formulae may not be what gets you fired up—but running out of cash isn't an issue any business owner wants to confront.

Keeping track of cash flow into and out of your organization means you have a more comprehensive knowledge of your firm's financial health. You can foresee cash flow issues and address them before they occur, and you may improve your operations so cash flow concerns become a thing of the past.

Chapter 7

Avoid compromise

Many claim that compromise is the key to a good relationship, a saying that is used in many situations, including business. Where it is important to compromise on some matters some are utterly non-negotiable in my opinion, believing that with specific subjects sticking by your guns is the only alternative.

Here are the 5 aspects of the business you should never compromise:

1: Never settle for an easier existence

In business people back down for an easy life, considering agreeing to be the only way to enjoy a working life free of difficulties. This is where I feel genuine business innovation must come into play, with success being something you have to battle for, not something that you just stumble into.

As they say, everything that is worth having is worth battling for, and this phrase has never been truer than in business.

2: Price

Where service and a fantastic staff are crucial cogs in your company wheel money is what makes the world go round. This is why it is crucial to never sell yourself too short, requiring you to earn a livelihood and retain the profits as high as possible. Too frequently I see business owners not having the guts to charge reasonably for their services, scared that they would lose clients if they boost rates up.

The key to pricing rests with justification, hence you must question yourself whether or not you can support a price rise.

3: Your morals

As an individual, you will apply principles that are embedded within your personality, sentiments, and beliefs that are set inside your mind. I have always thought that a company should be an extension of these strong ideas, with the essential principles of your business established by you. By doing so you construct a business that you will look at as 'your baby', having a personal link with your firm that will foster success.

4: Your personal life

Over the years I have discovered that it is crucial to take time off to spend with the family, with time away from work being helpful for both the health and happiness of yourself as well as your company. Sometimes you might be way too close to a project, distorting your perception of the boundaries and successes possible. By getting time off of the workplace you allow yourself to update your creativity, returning to said project with new eyes.

5: Standard of service

Many executives grow greedy as time goes on, thinking of themselves before their clients. Where price rises are not necessarily a negative thing Time is essential. In my view you have to make sure your service earns your consumers rather than the other way around, continually pushing to be a favorite alternative above your competition.

In conclusion, complacency should not be exhibited anywhere within business practice and you should constantly keep your eye on the ball, only compromise if it benefits yourself and your organization.

www.ingramcontent.com/pod-product-compliance
Lightning Source LLC
Chambersburg PA
CBHW050050260726
48658CB00005B/1863